OVERCOMING ADVERSITY

STEVIE WONDER

Tenley Williams

Introduction by James Scott Brady,
Trustee, the Center to Prevent Handgun Violence
Vice Chairman, the Brain Injury Foundation

Chelsea House Publishers
Philadelphia

CHELSEA HOUSE PUBLISHERS

EDITOR IN CHIEF Sally Cheney
DIRECTOR OF PRODUCTION Kim Shinners
PRODUCTION MANAGER Pamela Loos
ART DIRECTOR Sara Davis
SENIOR EDITOR John Ziff
PRODUCTION EDITOR Diann Grasse
LAYOUT 21st Century Publishing and Communications, Inc.

First Printing

1 3 5 7 9 8 6 4 2

The Chelsea House World Wide Web address is
http://www.chelseahouse.com

Library of Congress Cataloging-in-Publication Data

Williams, Tenley.
    Stevie Wonder / Tenley Williams ; introduction by James Scott Brady
        p. cm. — (Overcoming adversity)
    Discography: p.
    Includes bibliographical references and index.
    Summary: A biography of the blind composer, pianist, and singer whose musical
    ability, apparent since childhood, has earned him many awards.
    ISBN 0-7910-5903-0 (alk. paper)
       1. Wonder, Stevie—Juvenile literature. 2. Rock musicians—United States—
    Biography—Juvenile literature. [1. Wonder, Stevie. 2. Musicians. 3. Composers.
    4. African Americans—Biography. 5. Blind. 6. Physically handicapped.] I. Brady,
    James S. II Title. III. Series.

    ML3930.W65 W53 2002
    782.421644'092—dc21
       [B]   2001047595

STEVIE WONDER

CONTENTS

OVERCOMING ADVERSITY

ON FACING ADVERSITY

James Scott Brady

I GUESS IT'S a long way from a Centralia, Illinois, train yard to the George Washington University Hospital Trauma Unit. My dad was a yardmaster for the old Chicago, Burlington & Quincy Railroad. As a child, I used to get to sit in the engineer's lap and imagine what it was like to drive that train. I guess I always have liked being in the "driver's seat."

Years later, however, my interest turned from driving trains to driving campaigns. In 1979, former Texas governor John Connally hired me as a press secretary in his campaign for the American presidency. We lost the Republican primary to a former Hollywood star named Ronald Reagan. But I managed to jump over to the Reagan campaign. When Reagan was elected in 1980, I was "sitting in the catbird seat," as humorist James Thurber would say—poised to be named presidential press secretary. I held that title throughout the eight years of the Reagan administration. But not without one terrible, extended interruption.

It happened barely two months after the Reagan administration took office. I never even heard the shots. On March 30, 1981, my life went blank in an instant. In an attempt to assassinate President Reagan, John Hinckley Jr. armed himself with a "Saturday night special"—a low-quality, $29 pistol—and shot wildly as our presidential entourage exited a Washington hotel. One of the exploding bullets struck me just above the left eye. It shattered into a couple dozen fragments, some of which penetrated my skull and entered my brain.

The next few months of my life were a nightmare of repeated surgery, broken contact with the outside world, and a variety of medical complications. More than once, I was very close to death.

The next few years were filled with frustrating struggles to function with a paralyzed right side, struggles to speak and communicate.

To people who face and defeat daunting obstacles, "ambition" is not becoming wealthy or famous or winning elections or awards. Words like "ambition" and "achievement" and "success" take on very different meanings. The objective is just to live, to wake up every morning. The goals are not lofty; they are very ordinary.

My own heroes are ordinary folks—but they accomplish extraordinary things because they try. My greatest hero is my wife, Sarah. She's accomplished a lot of things in life, but two stand out. The first has been the way she has cared for me and our son since I was shot. A tremendous tragedy and burden was dropped unexpectedly into her life, totally beyond her control and without justification. She could have given up; instead, she focused her energies on preserving our family and returning our lives to normal as much as possible. Week by week, month by month, year by year, she has not reached for the miraculous, just for the normal. Yet in focusing on the normal, she has helped accomplish the miraculous.

Her other most remarkable accomplishment, to me, has been spearheading the effort to keep guns out of the hands of criminals and children in America. Opponents call her a "gun grabber"; I call her a national hero. And I am not alone.

After a seven-year battle, during which Sarah and I worked tirelessly to educate the public about the need for stronger gun laws, the Brady Bill became law in 1993. It was a victory, achieved in the face of tremendous opposition, that now benefits all Americans. From the time the law took effect through fall 1997, background checks had stopped 173,000 criminals and other high-risk purchasers from buying handguns, and the law has helped to reduce illegal gun trafficking.

Sarah was not pursuing fame, or even recognition. She simply started at one point—when our son, Scott, found a loaded handgun on the seat of a pickup truck and, thinking it was a toy, pointed it at Sarah.

Fortunately, no one was hurt. But seeing a gun nearly bring a second tragedy upon our family, Sarah became determined to do whatever she could to prevent senseless death and injury from guns.

Some people think of Sarah as a powerful political force. To me, she's the person who so many times fed me and helped me dress during my long years of recovery.

Overcoming obstacles is part of life, not just for people who are challenged by disabilities, illnesses, or tragedies, but for all people. No matter what the obstacle—fear, disability, prejudice, grief, or a difficulty that isn't likely to "just go away"—we can all work to make this world a better place.

Stevie Wonder, in a familiar posture after his recovery from a near-fatal automobile accident. Stevie's return to performing was greeted with critical acclaim and delirious enthusiasm from fans.

1

TRIUMPHANT RETURN

IN APRIL OF 1974 Stevie Wonder played his first American concert since suffering a near-fatal car accident just eight months earlier. Stepping onto the stage of New York City's Madison Square Garden, he offered the crowd a warm greeting to open the show. "I love you, hello!" he shouted to the fans packed into the arena. *Time* magazine described what for many was a magical scene:

> Sporting a mustache and his familiar dark glasses, he pointed toward heaven, then to his forehead and finally cut loose with a survivor's smile. From the balcony, loges and floor of the Garden came a roar—20,000 voices strong—of adulation, welcome and animal joy. . . . It was fine to hear a voice so long addicted to sweet soul now revel in husky, emotive blues growls. The pulsating climax came with an almost symphonic version of his "Living in the City," a black odyssey that begins in Mississippi and ends with the arrest of an innocent youth in New York. . . . Wonder topped that off by bringing out three fellow

blacks—Sly Stone, Eddie Kendricks and Roberta Flack—
for a reprise of "Superstition" and a rollicking, hand-
clapping, ear-piercing finale. . . .

Sitting up there onstage, his head bobbing and
weaving sightlessly as though trying to tune in on some
private radar of the mind, he recalls no one so much as
his old idol . . . Ray Charles.

Stevie takes any comparison to his idol as a great
compliment, and, like Charles, he strives to make each
show special. Even the Garden's notoriously bad acoustics
could not diminish the power of the performance or the
control Stevie exercised over the production.

Stevie played uninterrupted for one hour and 45
minutes. He began with a leisurely improvisation on
"Contusion" and moved immediately into some of his
most famous songs, such as "Superwoman" and "Keep
on Running." Performing with his backup group,
Wonderlove, consisting of three women singers and an
instrumental quartet, Stevie himself manned the three-
tiered instrumental construct called an ARP synthesizer.
The biggest surprise of the night may have been that he
had brought something new to his singing. The sweet,
soulful sound of his voice had a new timbre, a huskier,
more emotive blues quality that turned light ballads such
as "For Once in My Life" into what one critic called
"emotional soul food." At just 23 years old, this slender,
six-foot superstar—what the music business calls a
"monster"—was an artist who played to sellout crowds
and whose recordings transcended musical categories
and audience distinctions. He had been a professional
musician for 11 years, and no one knew better how to
take command of a stage.

The Garden show reached a climax with "Living for the
City." The audience was on its feet, singing with him, their
movements synchronized to what he calls his "blindisms":
the bobbing and weaving movements of his head that, he

says, release his excess energies. By the time Stevie and his invited guests played "Superstition," the fans were dancing on their seats.

But this fabulous performance nearly didn't take place. The life and career of this incredible performer and musical innovator was almost cut short on August 6, 1973, on the way to a tour date in Durham, North Carolina. Stevie was asleep in the passenger seat of a car driven by his cousin, John Harris. As Harris attempted to pass a logging truck that had stopped without warning, a log broke loose from the truck and crashed through the windshield of the car, striking Stevie in the head. Pulled bloody and unconscious from the wreck, he remained in a coma for several days with a broken skull and a brain contusion. Friends and family knelt beside his bed to pray and sing his songs to him, hoping to reach him, to keep him alive. His friend and publicist Ira Tucker knelt close to Stevie's ear. "God is gonna show you higher ground," he sang from Stevie's song *Higher Ground.* "He's the only friend you have around." At last, Stevie began to slowly move his fingers in time to the music. Finally regaining consciousness, he is said to have joked, "I can see! I can see! . . . Just kidding."

Three months later, despite doctors' orders not to exert himself, Stevie performed and acted as emcee at a homecoming benefit for North Carolina's Shaw University, of which he is a trustee. Writing music and planning the production of his next tour as he recuperated, Stevie focused upon performing again. He had gained insight from the accident, as well as a new perspective on his life and a determination to accomplish all he could. "I've come to realize my time on earth is not yet done and there are things to do. I want to travel," he said. "I believe I only have one iota of the knowledge I'd like to have when I leave this life."

He never complained during his recuperation from that terrible accident in North Carolina, but one can imagine how terrifying it must have been for Stevie Wonder to believe, even for a moment, that his musical career might be over. But Stevie never stopped believing that he had much more to accomplish in his life.

His recovery was nothing short of miraculous. He began focusing on his music from the moment he regained consciousness, readying himself for a return to his concert schedule. Just six months after his accident, Stevie was back where he wanted to be—on stage.

His very first live comeback performances took place in England. "Stevie Wonder Returns with a Synthesized Howl," proclaimed *Rolling Stone* magazine in February 1974, after his two sold-out London concerts at the Rainbow Theatre, which had been artistic triumphs. Though the audience could not see them, scars from the accident were still visible on his face. Nor did fans know that Stevie was taking an anticonvulsive medication, or that his sense of smell had been forever impaired. Paul McCartney, Eric Clapton, Ringo Starr, Pete Townshend, David Bowie, and the Staple Singers were among those who had come to hear the work of a respected fellow musician, a man at the forefront of black popular music.

The crowd roared with respect and admiration as Stevie was led onto the London stage. When he was seated at the ARP synthesizer, the applause finally subsided as he began the improvisational half-hour piece called "Contusion," in which he introduced all the musicians onstage with him, each of whom performed a brief solo. Accompanied, as always, by Wonderlove, which would be joined periodically by many brass players, an electric violinist, and flautist Bobbi Humphrey, Stevie focused on selections from his newest albums, *Talking Book* and *Innervisions,* an album that has since been called his masterpiece. He also sang songs the crowd already knew and loved from "two thousand years ago," as he put it, including "Signed, Sealed, Delivered (I'm Yours)," a song on which his

mother had collaborated, and "Uptight (Everything's Alright)," the song that had become his signature piece.

To those closest to him, his comeback performances not only marked Stevie's return from the horrific accident, but also celebrated his amazing success. A black musician who started his musical career performing for black audiences, he had established himself as a musician with no musical barriers, an artist for all listeners. He had also proven himself to be concerned about more than his own career. By the time of the London concerts, he had become a consistent supporter of numerous humanitarian efforts. His concerts and performances on behalf of educational programs, the inner-city poor, international causes, and

An informal get-together with Paul McCartney after one of Stevie's 1974 comeback concerts in London would lead to a long-term friendship and collaboration with the former Beatle. The two are seen here in Los Angeles on November 28, 1989, performing their hit "Ebony and Ivory."

the blind brought him worldwide respect and admiration.

The London audience, like many throughout his career, seemed to love his ballads such as "Visions," "All in Love Is Fair," and "Sky Blue Afternoon." With each song, the crowd responded with as much warmth as Stevie himself was putting forth onstage. Wonderlove gamely followed Stevie's improvisations as he caught them by surprise with his digressions from the rehearsed arrangements. "It *couldn't* be slick," Stevie later explained, "because we hadn't performed in a long time. But I wasn't worried. . . . Wonderlove is very perceptive. Musically and spiritually, they're on the same level with me." But Stevie always sets the level, and he is always in charge onstage, drawing the music together according to his own plan, his own inner vision.

Stevie left the stage with a "howl" produced by the synthesizers he had set to end one of his and his fans' favorite songs, "Superstition." He later explained, "To me, 'Superstition' is such an exciting tune that I can't just end it. 'Superstition' brings back thousands of *outasight* memories, so I just put the synthesizer on and split."

The song ended his second encore, which lasted 90 minutes, and the audience rose to give Stevie the second standing ovation of the night. Stevie just didn't want to stop. "The first show I was feeling the people, getting warm," he said the next day. "I was feeling their presence. . . . I hadn't planned on doing the two encores; they were in response to the people." Then, displaying his sense of humor, he asked, "They were standing, weren't they?"

Eating his post-performance snack of chocolate chip cookies and hot tea, he talked with Ira Tucker about getting together with Paul McCartney the next day. They would meet at a recording studio, Stevie decided, and "just mess around." Messing around with Paul McCartney would prove to be a fruitful way to spend some time. They would participate together in concerts for many humanitarian causes over the years, and

The cover of Fulfillingness' First Finale. *Many of the songs on the album reflected Stevie's emotions upon surviving a near-death experience.*

Stevie eventually recorded his own versions of several Beatles songs.

A year after the accident, Stevie was still recovering from his injuries and taking Dilantin to control seizures. His next album, *Fulfillingness' First Finale,* reflected his deeper focus on things spiritual and proved that his artistry had not been diminished by the accident. While it includes both the political, funk anthem "You Haven't Done Nothin'" and the dance tune "Boogie on Reggae Woman," the album is in many ways more thoughtful and reflective than his previous albums, Stevie explained, "because I guess that's how it would be when you are as close to death as I was."

Stevie's musical gift was evident at a young age. Seen here without his trademark sunglasses, a youthful Stevie plays the bongo drums.

2

BEGINNINGS

ON MAY 13, 1950, Stevland Hardaway Judkins was born in Saginaw, Michigan. He was the son of Lula Mae Morris Hardaway. She gave him the name Stevland Morris so that he would not have to carry the surname of his absentee father. He was not blind at birth, as many people think. Born prematurely, he spent the first 56 days of his life in a hospital incubator. Too much oxygen was accidentally pumped into the incubator, and his eyes were irreparably damaged. "A girl who was born that same day was also put into the incubator and she died," he later remarked. "I personally think I'm lucky to be alive."

With no husband or father for her kids at home—in addition to Stevie, Lula also had two other sons, Milton and Calvin—she cleaned houses to support her young family. In 1954, she decided to reunite with Paul Hardaway, the father of Milton and Calvin, and moved with her boys to Detroit. Stevie's younger brothers Larry and Timothy, along with a sister, Renee, would later complete this close and always supportive family.

Stevie grew up comfortably in what he likes to call "upper-lower-class circumstances," listening to the city's most popular radio stations and identifying early on with another blind singer—Ray Charles. With his transistor radio usually pressed close to his ear, he explored the neighborhood with Milton and Calvin. Despite his blindness, Stevie's world was filled with music, days at Fitzgerald Elementary School, the companionship of adventurous brothers, and a neighborhood ripe for a curious child's exploration. There were bikes to ride, trees to climb, games to play, and mischief to be fearlessly and enthusiastically wrought. Because of his family, Stevie was able to live a normal childhood, developing a sense of independence. "They would tell me what was happening and where things were, and give me a sense of a parameter," Stevie recalled. "My mother never said, 'Let me walk with you, I don't want you to walk down these stairs; you might fall.'" She would caution him, but sometimes allow him to learn for himself.

One memorable day, Stevie learned about how a dog may take a person by surprise. His mother had warned him not to go off the porch. "I must have been three years old, and I found my way off the porch, as you know kids do," Stevie remembers. "I was walking around off the porch, and I stepped in something. . . . My mom said, 'I told you.'"

His brothers also strengthened his sense of independence and his confidence to do what all the other kids were doing. "There were kids who used to make fun of me and say, 'Here comes the blind man,'" Stevie recalls. "But I was too busy wanting to have fun to worry about that. Having brothers like I did, I would always want to do everything they did. If they jumped off the porch, I would want to do that too. They just gave me the freedom of being independent, of discovering things."

But his brothers and friends also made sure he didn't

get hurt. "I had friends who cared and wouldn't let me get into any bad situations," Stevie says. "I wanted to do every single thing that a sighted person did, and between my friends and my brothers they would make sure I didn't do anything crazy."

In return, Stevie has given a lot to his brothers and his entire family. All his brothers have worked as Stevie's assistants and bodyguards throughout his professional life. "They keep him out of trouble," a friend observes. "It's a beautiful thing. It's a family working together. Stevie has been a very positive influence on them all."

Stevie often tried to comfort his mother and alleviate her worries about his safety and his future. He was always assuring her that she need not worry about him, that he was happy with himself as he was. But Lula agonized over her son's blindness. She feared that the double burden of blindness and society's racism would make his life sad and difficult. Lula explored every way available to find a cure, a remedy for Stevie's blindness. She prayed, consulted doctors, and even sought the help of faith healers, but nothing could change her son's condition. However, Lula knew that Stevie had a gift for music, and she encouraged him to work with that gift.

By the time he was two years old, Stevie's musical talent had begun to emerge. No one else in the family seemed to have anything like it; Stevie's gift was all his own. After listening to her son banging out rhythms with his hands and with spoons on tabletops, pots, and pans, Lula came home one day with a set of cardboard drums. Her small son quickly wore them out. At age five, a four-note harmonica from his uncle opened another musical door, and Stevie never went anywhere without it, coaxing tunes from it at every opportunity. At a picnic where a blues band played, Stevie kept time with spoons. The drummer, impressed with the small boy's timing and enthusiasm, pulled him onto his lap and let him play the drums. The picnickers loved him, and Stevie earned his first pay as a musician—two quarters.

Another story tells of family members gathering in the kitchen and dropping coins onto the table as everyone took turns asking, "What is it, Stevie?" He was only five years old, but Stevie would call out "quarter," "dime," "nickel," or "penny," and only pennies and nickels ever gave him trouble. Precocious and already inventive, the little boy's sensitivity to sound was being honed into a "musician's ear" that would soon become the most important part of his life.

Of course, music education can be extremely expensive, and the family had little money to spare. But the neighborhood where Lula was raising her family proved to be full of unexpected resources. Soon the entire community recognized Stevie's talent and responded to the needs of this pint-sized musical dynamo in their midst. A local barber gave him his first real harmonica. As Stevie drew melodies from it, the sound and style that would become distinctively his own began to develop. Next, the Lion's Club supplied a set of drums; then, the lady next door let Stevie come over to play her piano. When he was seven, she moved away and left it for him; Stevie could hardly wait for that piano to be moved into his house. He learned everything he could about all the instruments, always looking for new and better ways to make music. Playing for neighbors and at a local church, Stevie became a neighborhood sensation.

Everyone around him recognized that young Stevie also had a fine voice. In the Whitestone Baptist Church junior choir, he began singing lead parts. Outside of church, however, he liked to sing rhythm and blues rather than religious music. As far as the church elders were concerned, Stevie may have had an extraordinary voice and a musical gift, but popular music and gospel music were not compatible genres. One day, after a church elder had heard him singing rock and roll songs on his front porch, Stevie was quietly asked to leave the choir.

He may have been disappointed, but he was not

discouraged. Being ejected from the choir didn't stop him from singing or from making music; Stevie continued to sing and play the pop music he heard on the radio, soaking up the influences of artists like B. B. King, Johnny Ace, Jackie Wilson, the Coasters, La Vern Baker, Bobby Bland, and, of course, Ray Charles. The gospel music of the Staple Singers was also a big influence. "I listened to as much and as many different kinds of music as possible," he said later. "The radio was one of my best friends." By the time he was nine years old, Stevie was playing the harmonica up and down the neighborhood streets and singing with friends or just by himself.

After he was placed in a school with special classes for the blind, Stevie learned to speak more clearly and to read Braille, a system of tiny raised dots that is read with the fingers. But, perhaps most difficult of all, he had to learn how to show emotion. Since he had never seen anyone laugh or cry, Stevie didn't know how to express feelings in ways that everyone could understand. If his life were to someday move outside his circle of loving family and friends, he would need more skills than his music; he would need to know how to relate to the world in an understandable and socially acceptable way.

Stevie also learned something else at school: that because of his disability and his race, many people didn't expect him to amount to much. Some teachers said that despite his education, despite his talent, and despite his desire to learn, he would end up with a career of making pot holders! Another teacher told Stevie that he had three strikes against him: he was blind, black, and broke. At the time these were all formidable limitations, but Stevie never treated them as barriers; they were just circumstances. His life had music, family, and adventure, and he reveled in all of it. He thought he might grow up to be a minister or an electrician. Life was full of possibilities, as far as Stevie was concerned. His love of music and performing, however, soon began to eclipse every other interest.

When he was nine, Stevie formed a duo with his best friend, John Glover. As "Steve and John," the boys sang and played popular songs they heard on the radio, imitating other artists. Stevie played bongos and sang; John played guitar and sang harmony. "We did a lot of the songs of the fifties and sixties," Stevie recalled, "We did 'Once Upon a Time' and 'Why Do Fools Fall in Love?' . . . We sang around Detroit. We did 'Stairway to Heaven.' We used to do 'She's Not a Bad Girl,' a Smokey Robinson and the Miracles song. And we did another Smokey song, '[Shop Around].' I used to love to do the imitations of Jackie Wilson, and it was crazy because, when I became aware of how Jackie Wilson performed—I heard he was a very exciting performer—I used to do all kinds of flips and stuff. I was about nine or ten years old then."

John kept pestering his older brother, telling him that Stevie was something special, that he had to hear him. At last, John got his cousin to listen to his talented friend. John's cousin happened to be Ronnie White of the group Smokey Robinson and the Miracles. When White heard Stevie perform the Miracles' "Lonely Boy," he arranged a meeting for him with Brian Holland, a talent scout for Hitsville U.S.A. Records. In the company's Detroit recording studios, Stevie's life turned completely and forever to music.

Holland was so excited by what he heard from Stevie that he interrupted Berry Gordy, the president and founder of Hitsville (soon to be renamed Motown), during breakfast to urge him to sign a contract with this astonishing young performer. Skeptical but interested, Gordy came to hear the 10-year-old. "He was singing, playing the bongos and blowing on a harmonica. His voice didn't knock me out, but his harmonica playing did. Something about him was infectious," Gordy later wrote in his autobiography. "I said 'Boy! That kid's a wonder!' and the name stuck." Another story suggests that Clarence Paul nicknamed him "Little Stevie" and everyone else accepted it. Regardless

Stevie performs with Jackie Wilson, a singer he numbers among the many diverse influences that have shaped his music.

of the details, Stevland Morris quickly became known professionally as Little Stevie Wonder. His uncle, Willie Morris, adopted him to protect his earnings from his absent father, and Lula Mae signed a five-year contract for her son, now 11 years old.

Stevie went to the studio every day after attending classes at the Michigan School for the Blind that were arranged to accommodate his professional schedule. Esther Gordy Edwards, who was Stevie's personal manager in the early 1960s, remembered him as an energetic youngster. "Motown had eight houses up and down Grand Boulevard [in Detroit]," she recalled, "and

Stevie greets a Motown fan outside the record label's Detroit headquarters, Hitsville U.S.A.

he would be up and down the street, up and down in each one of them." But not all the older musicians were thrilled to see the "little boy wonder" with tons of talent. "He was a pest!" said Clarence Paul. "He'd come by at 3 every day after school and stay until dark. He'd play every instrument in the place and bust in on you when you was [recording] somebody."

Stevie also became known for having a great sense of humor and pulling some astounding pranks. In the studio, he might ask another musician, "Man, can I borrow your car? I have some runs to make." No one was off-limits for his practical jokes. For example, one day he called a secretary and, imitating Berry Gordy's distinctive voice, ordered a tape recorder for that "great new artist," Stevie Wonder. But no one could be angry with Stevie for long because he was always just one of the guys. "You never looked at him as being handicapped," said Smokey Robinson. "I recall when we used to take Motortown Revues to places like the Apollo [in New York City] and theaters like that and his dressing room would be on the fourth floor. By the second or third day he was running around backstage at the Apollo just like everybody else, like he could see."

Not everyone, however, treated Stevie just like everybody else. "I think back, unfortunately, on the ignorance that some people had about blindness and people who are blind. . . ." Stevie says. "[T]here was a little girl I used to like, and I would go visit her. She lived with her grandparents, who were very polite to me. But, as soon as I would leave, they would always give her a whuppin' for being with a kid who was blind. They thought if we ever got married when we grew up, and had a baby, the baby would be blind. [My blindness] is not something that is hereditary, and they just didn't know."

In August 1962 Stevie's first single release, "I Call It Pretty Music (But Old People Call It the Blues)," didn't make the Hot 100, but it did make an impression. Stevie's next two singles, "Little Water Boy" and "Contract On Love," released at the end of the year, didn't make the charts either. His first two albums, *The Jazz Soul of Little Stevie* and *Tribute to Uncle Ray,* did not set the pop world on fire either. But his live performance of "Fingertips" at the Regal Theater in Chicago made musical history.

Stevie had already recorded "Fingertips," a song written by Clarence Paul and Henry Crosby, in the studio for *The Jazz Soul of Little Stevie.* And, of course, it was included in the repertoire for his live performances. At the Chicago concert, as Paul led him from the stage after his performance, Stevie broke free and began singing

"Fingertips" again. It was unusual for Stevie to resist leaving the stage after performing. "I used to pick him up and carry him off—until he got too heavy," Paul recalled. But this time, the chemistry onstage was right for an extraordinary encore performance. The bass player had already left the stage, but a bassist who played for singer Mary Wells began to accompany Stevie's performance. "What key? What key?" the bassist asked frantically. This lively exchange was accidentally left in the final recording. "We're not sure why the record was such a big hit," Berry Gordy wrote in his autobiography. "There are certain kinds of mistakes I love."

Stevie was living an exciting dream, touring with the Temptations, Smokey Robinson, Marvin Gaye, and other great Motown artists. "I probably was excited to be just having fun," Stevie says.

> I wasn't thinking about it as my livelihood. I would dread leaving [to go] on the road, 'cause I loved being home with my brothers and sister, then I would hate leaving the road. Then I would dread going to school. But being on the road was incredible. Marvin Gaye was a very well-read man, so he and Smokey would be on the bus having discussions about the Bible, Greek mythology, Egyptian history, playing different kinds of music.

Life on the road is difficult in many ways for everyone who tours, but "[e]veryone over 11 was my parent," Stevie remembers. "Clarence Paul loved me like his own son, Esther Edwards, Berry Gordy's sister Ardena Johnson, all the musicians and artists watched over me."

In 1963 "Fingertips—Part 2" was released as a single and remained number one on the singles chart for 15 weeks, selling over 1 million copies. It was the first in-concert pop single ever to do so. The success of "Fingertips" surprised everyone, including the Motown executives, because it wasn't an elaborate studio production like all other Motown releases. Even after this success, however, they still weren't sure how to market their 12-year-old protégé.

Meanwhile, at age 12, Stevie was enjoying life at the Michigan School for the Blind in Lansing, Michigan. He found a lifelong friend in J. J. Jackson, a student at the school. "I'll never forget the first day he arrived," remembers Jackson. "He had just had his first million-selling hit, and all these hordes of kids were buzzing around waiting for him. After meeting him, all the kids said the same thing—he's a star, but also just a regular guy. He fits right in. That was impressive, and he's still the same way."

At the Michigan School for the Blind, Stevie lived in a dormitory and had a curfew. Each night, the night guard performed a bed check. Then, when the steps of the guard sounded far enough away, the boys would climb out their windows and slip over to the little store across the street for pop and chips. "On one occasion," recalls Jackson, "it got a little confusing. Stevie accidentally climbed back inside the dorm through the wrong window and into the wrong room. I guess the night guard heard some noises, because we heard him starting to come up toward our room. We thought Stevie was outside, so we started to call to him softly. Stevie had realized he was in the wrong room because the furniture was all in a different place." His friends called to him and managed to get him—and themselves—back in their room before the guard came around again. "We saved his skin that night," laughs Jackson. Years later Jackson would become Stevie's computer systems adviser and consultant. He found the optical scanning software that makes it possible for Stevie and other blind individuals to read documents independently.

Ted Hall, a teacher from the Michigan School for the Blind, was assigned to accompany Stevie on the road and during long recording sessions so he could keep up with his studies. Hall also taught him techniques for being more independent, such as counting the number of steps to the microphone so he wouldn't always need to be led out onto the stage. But his real job often seemed to be just trying to keep up with Stevie.

On May 21, 1963, what would become Stevie's first successful album was released: *Little Stevie Wonder, the 12-Year-Old Genius.* (He was 13 by the time it came out.) In addition to "Fingertips, Pts. 1 & 2," the album, recorded live, included "A Tribute to Ray Charles," one of the most important influences on Stevie's music.

With "Fingertips," Stevie was the first artist to simultaneously reach number one on the Hot 100 and the Rhythm and Blues (R & B) singles chart, and *12-Year-Old Genius* was on the Billboard album chart at the same time. Then, for the next two years, none of his recordings would come near to the success of "Fingertips." His next album, *Work Out, Stevie, Work Out,* was never released, and two subsequent albums, *With a Song in My Heart* (December 1963) and *Stevie at the Beach* (June 1964), yielded dismal sales figures. Some Motown executives thought it might be a good time to tear up Stevie's contract and turn their attention to more popular and profitable artists. "I understood where they were coming from," Stevie said years later. "They basically felt that I was not really making any money for the company. My voice was hanging . . . they didn't know what to do." His voice was changing, dropping from a little boy's soprano to a more mature timbre. Motown producer and songwriter Sylvia Moy urged the executives to give Stevie's music one more chance. Inspired by a musical phrase she had heard him play, she collaborated with producer Henry Cosby and Stevie on what would become one of his most enduring hits, "Uptight (Everything's Alright)."

In July 1964 the studio decided to drop the "Little" from Stevie's professional name when he appeared, along with Frankie Avalon and Annette Funicello, in the forgettable movies *Bikini Beach* and *Muscle Beach*

Party. Stevie had no interest in pursuing a movie career, and Motown executives, fortunately, had no interest in encouraging him to do so. They had another objective: Motown wanted to change the face—and the *color* of the face—of American pop music.

During the 1960s new sounds were emerging in rock music. The Beach Boys, Bob Dylan, and Simon and

Though barely a teenager, Stevie shared billing with some of Motown's biggest stars at the famed Apollo Theater in New York.

Frankie Avalon, Stevie Wonder, and Annette Funicello in a scene from the forgettable 1964 film Muscle Beach Party. *Stevie's acting career would be short lived.*

Garfunkel were among the artists making a strong swerve out of the rock and roll of the 1950s toward a new sound. The black musicians honing their talents in Detroit, including the Four Tops, Sam Cooke, Marvin Gaye, the Temptations, the Supremes, and Martha and the Vandellas, were attracting white audiences with a sound becoming known as "soul" music. Recalling Stevie's early career, columnist Ken McIntyre wrote in the *Washington Times* of the Motown sound that Stevie Wonder was helping to create: It was "a blend of rock and rhythm and blues—

'the Sound of Young America'—that compelled white, suburban teens to embrace a beat made by urban blacks. The music's undeniable appeal inspired a sort of color blindness on the airwaves and jukeboxes of a nation still largely segregated by race."

Stevie gets a hug from his mom upon graduating from the Michigan School for the Blind, January 1968. He would soon take control of his musical career.

3

GRADUATION

IN MARCH OF 1965, Stevie performed with other Motown musicians in a 21-show tour of the United Kingdom. He had become an international star, and "Uptight (Everything's Alright)" had become a worldwide hit.

From 1965 through 1970, Stevie Wonder was marketed to the public just like the other Motown stars. Company executives decided what he would record and which movies he would appear in; his albums were a studio-approved mix of conventional soul music and pop standards. In the United States, "Uptight," very much in the Motown mainstream, began a run of Top 40 hits for Stevie that would continue for the next six years.

However, Stevie did not want to be classified as a "black" or "soul" musician. In response to his dissatisfaction with their businesslike restrictions and to the firmness of his humanitarian interests, Motown allowed Stevie to record Bob Dylan's "Blowin' in the Wind." The single reached number nine on the pop charts in 1966. One writer stated that the song, which started as a "civil rights song beloved by the folksingers, comes out as a rocking soul anthem with much militancy added." But Stevie would have to wait a little longer to explore social issues in his own songwriting.

Stevie was a regular on the *Billboard* Top 10 in the '60s with numerous songs, including "A Place in the Sun," "I Was Made to Love Her," "For Once in My Life," "My Cherie Amour," and "Shoo-Be-Doo-Be-Doo-Da-Day." In 1968, using the pseudonym Eivets Rednow, he released an album of the same name that contained harmonica music, including a version of composer Burt Bacharach's "Alfie." In case listeners didn't recognize Stevie's harmonica playing and unique voice, spelling the names backward revealed his identity.

But Stevie had high ambitions and even higher standards for his music. By 1967 he was cowriting most of his singles and collaborating on songs for other Motown musicians. He cowrote the hit "The Tears of a Clown" for Smokey Robinson and the Miracles, and he produced and cowrote "It's a Shame" for the Spinners.

In January 1968, Stevie graduated with a high school diploma from the Michigan School for the Blind. A year and a half later, he was invited by President Richard Nixon to come to the White House to receive an award for his charitable work on behalf of the handicapped.

On September 14, 1970, Stevie married Syreeta Wright, a singer and songwriter at Motown. Although the marriage would last only until 1972, their personal and professional friendship would endure. Because of Stevie's efforts to keep his personal life private, details about his family are sketchy. However, it is known that he eventually fathered two children with Yolanda Simmons, and later had a third child with vocalist Melody McCulley. His children are named Aisha, Keita, and Mumtaz.

Stevie won his first Grammy award in 1971 for *Signed, Sealed & Delivered,* which was honored as the Best Soul Album. With this album Stevie finally convinced Motown to let him play his music his own way. In production, he argued with the album's half dozen producers and usually won. He

Stevie Wonder and Syreeta Wright shortly after their wedding ceremony, September 14, 1970. The marriage would end in divorce.

helped write 7 of the album's 12 songs, including the title track, cowritten with his mother and Syreeta Wright.

On May 13, 1971, his 21st birthday, Stevie's contract with Motown expired. Rather than re-sign with the company that gave him his start, as the studio executives expected, he planned not to sign with any studio. Instead, he financed the recording of two albums of his own material. At age 21, Stevie wanted control over every aspect of his music. But there had been many advantages to being a teenage musician whose career was being directed for him: He had learned what he needed to know from many of the most accomplished and successful musicians, singers, songwriters, and producers in the business. He had led a sheltered life, able to hone his formidable talent under the guidance and protection of Berry Gordy and Motown. He had been able to avoid the bad advice and the worse company that ruined the careers of many young entertainers. Stevie had grown up, as one writer noted, "whole and wholesome" with the development of soul music, and he was eager to bring his talents as a singer, multi-instrumentalist, lyricist, and composer to his own projects. "Motown did a pretty good job," he explained later. "But I basically wanted to do more, I felt I didn't want to slide into one bag. And I didn't know the significance of having my own publishing [company]. Music changes, and if you're in the line of change and don't move, you get trampled."

Wisely for Stevie, however, and happily for Motown, he had signed another contract with Motown as a staff writer. This contract, separate from his contract as a solo artist, allowed him to write and collaborate on songs for other performers. Harry Weinger, a producer and friend of Stevie, relates a conversation with the late Clarence Paul, Stevie's Motown mentor, who described the way music was never outside of Stevie's creative vision: "Stevie was always coming up with things—writing on the plane, the bus, the way to the studio. With Stevie, the groove, the track came first. Stevie always delivered a bad groove. We'd build with words on that."

By 1970 he had written songs for the Marvelettes, Diana Ross & the Supremes, the Contours, Marvin Gaye, Martha Reeves & the Vandellas, the Temptations, Ramsey Lewis, the Spinners, the Four Tops, and Smokey Robinson and the Miracles. As time went on, there was always a Motown artist ready to perform a song written by Stevie Wonder. He was astonished when Ray Charles won an award in 1975 for his performance of "Living for the City," a song Stevie had written. "I still can't believe it," Stevie said in an interview. "That song was all right but, I mean, he deserves something even better than that. I feel that there will never ever be an award great enough to give Ray Charles. He's opened the door for so many hearts. . . . I really feel that."

No longer under the artistic control of Motown as a solo artist, Stevie was ready to strike out on his own. He moved into a recording studio in New York City and formed his own recording company, Taurus Productions, and a publishing company, Black Bull Music. (Many people think that a bull embodies the type of determination and power that Stevie brings to his work.) He hired a staff and began work on a new album, intent on producing a new sound.

Electronic music, also called synthesized music, had begun to interest Stevie a great deal. Throughout his entire life he had been acutely tuned in to the quality and possibilities of new sounds in music. Besides the electric guitar and a small number of effects to be achieved in a studio, electronic composition was as yet unknown in soul or pop music because electronic instruments weren't widely available. So Stevie acquired and learned to play a Moog synthesizer, an electronic keyboard developed in 1964 that could produce just about any sound he wanted. Nothing like the Moog had ever been used before in soul music. With the assistance of engineers Malcolm Cecil and Robert Margouleff, his pioneering work with the synthesizer brought a new dimension to the pop music business. But for Stevie it was more than just a new sound. It was, he said, "a tool to work with [the] sounds I had in my mind, since I couldn't do notation and give a musician the part to do."

In order to play all the instruments on his recordings, Stevie taped each part, then combined them by a process called overdubbing. He sometimes worked 50 hours without stopping, and he eventually recorded more than 200 tracks. The result was the album entitled *Music of My Mind,* a collection of original songs composed and arranged with the help of keyboard technology, synthesizers, and computers. He also used many of these new production techniques on the album *Syreeta.*

Before releasing *Music of My Mind,* Stevie decided to sign another contract with Motown. In a music-industry first, Berry Gordy agreed to some surprising terms. Stevie would record at Taurus Productions and Motown would market his work. Profits would be split evenly. Stevie would be free to record his own music his own way. After signing the new contract, Stevie celebrated by releasing *Where I'm Coming From* in April 1971.

Where I'm Coming From was actually the last album Stevie recorded for Motown as a minor, before creating his own publishing company. The title seems to acknowledge his professional roots in the organization that gave him the chance to establish himself as an artist. It also declares a fresh sense of independence and a new direction for the innovative young artist. But once again, Stevie had to scratch and climb back onto the charts. Not until the release of *Music of My Mind* in March 1972 did he have even a modest hit with "Superwoman," a song about his relationship with Syreeta.

Then came the album *Talking Book,* which has been regarded as signaling Stevie Wonder's transformation from child genius to confident grown-up. On the cover of the album, he appeared in elaborate African braids and, for the first time, without a pair of sunglasses to hide his sightless eyes. In the cover's first printing the album's title appeared in Braille so that blind fans could read the print. Stevie would remain an innovator in applying new technology and devices to aid blind individuals.

Stevie was also eager to incorporate broader, more universal topics into his music. *Talking Book* was released in 1972 to critical praise as a "colorful musical painting," an extraordinary description of the work of a musician who had never seen colors. The single "Superstition" was a popular hit, and the ballad "You Are the Sunshine of My Life" won three Grammy awards. With *Talking Book,* Stevie had moved away from the romantic formula of songs about breaking up and making up. Beautiful ballads can still be found with "You and I" and "I Believe When I Fall in Love It Will Be Forever." But with songs such as "Big Brother," Stevie began to express the views, hopes, and fears of many Americans, particularly black Americans. Some of his most successful songs have been about issues of black cultural pride, brotherhood, spiritual growth, and the ongoing struggle for social justice.

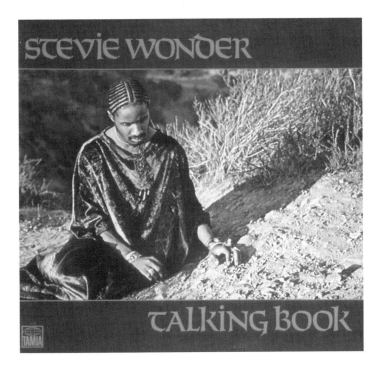

Many view the 1972 release Talking Book *as a landmark in Stevie's career. The album contained one of his biggest hits, "Superstition" and featured Stevie without sunglasses on the cover.*

After *Talking Book* had been recorded, Motown was particularly interested in "Superstition," a song that company executives believed would be a surefire hit single. The only problem was that Stevie had already promised guitarist Jeff Beck that he could record the song. Releasing "Superstition" on the album was one thing, but releasing it as a single marked it forever as Stevie's song. Beck was furious. At first, however, it seemed that there was no audience for "Superstition." When Stevie debuted the song at Harlem's Apollo Theater, the audience actually booed! "People weren't ready for it," Stevie said. "They wanted to hear 'Signed, Sealed, Delivered' and I can understand that because that is what they heard for the most part on the radio."

But the Apollo audience did not have the final word. "Superstition" rose to the top of the music charts. With his next number one hit, "You Are the Sunshine of My Life," Stevie Wonder produced what has been called an American standard, and he was well on his way to a very successful career.

With the release of Innervisions, *Stevie's appeal began to cross racial boundaries. The album sold more than 1 million copies and garnered the performer three Grammy Awards, including Best Album, in 1974.*

4

INNER VISION

IN THE FALL of 1972—a year marked by tense race relations, the winding down of the Vietnam War, and the beginning of the infamous Watergate scandal—Stevie joined John Lennon and Yoko Ono in a concert at Madison Square Garden. "Superstition," released in October 1972, became a number one hit, its "trust no one" message a timely reflection of the social and political climate of the day. A ballad, "You Are the Sunshine of My Life," released in February 1973, quickly went to the top of the charts too. Motown decided that it was time for Stevie to actively conquer a national audience. It was time for the wider world to hear what Stevie could do—and he was more than ready.

With Wonderlove, Stevie joined the Rolling Stones on their 50-city tour in the spring of 1973. Music critic Leonard Pitts Jr. said the show was "light years away from the teenybopper tour they had done [together] almost 10 years earlier." Stevie was already an established star with black audiences, but white music fans now took notice and gave him an enthusiastic reception when he joined Mick Jagger onstage to sing the Stones' famous single "Satisfaction." The Stones have always acknowledged the influence of American soul music, blues, and jazz on their own music, and Jagger and Stevie felt at home onstage together. The crowd loved it.

But the Stones' lifestyle, both on and off the road, came as a shock to Stevie. The drugs, liquor, and late hours, the parade of strangers through their rooms and their lives, and the media looking for ever more salacious scandal, were aspects of touring and the rock-and-roll life that had never been part of his own. "By rock standards," a reviewer remarked at the time, "Stevie is square. He does not drink; he has smoked pot only twice"—and of that experience, Stevie declared, "It scared me to death." But this wider audience, whose appreciation of Stevie's work crossed racial boundaries, was beginning to embody his dream of social and political brotherhood and love. His songs reflected his belief in our human capacity for compassion and for change.

On the album *Innervisions,* released in August 1973, Stevie addressed social and political themes in the songs "Living for the City" and "Higher Ground." The song "Living for the City" was one of the first soul hits to include both a political message and, in a process called "sampling," recordings of the sounds of the streets—voices, buses, traffic, and sirens—mixed with the music produced in the studio. The effect is to make African-American city experience more immediate for the listener. The music seems, in a way, to accompany life as it is being lived—outside the concert hall or the quiet listening space of one's own room. Critics have called *Innervisions* a masterpiece, a definitive work that transcends the barriers between blacks and whites. In transcending these barriers, however, Stevie never sacrificed or lost the power of the black experience in shaping his music or his message.

"Living for the City" tells the story of a young black man, full of what should be the most reasonable optimism,

who comes to New York City from a poor, working-class home in Mississippi. "Whoa. Just like I pictured it," he marvels. In the wrong place at the wrong time, he is sentenced to prison for 10 years. The music, controlled and melodic, contrasts sharply with the power of the terrible picture Stevie paints in the lyrics.

"Higher Ground" is a danceable piece with a political message and a sense of progress toward the ideals of reaching a higher level of social and personal conscience.

Stevie, who toured with the Rolling Stones in 1973, joins lead singer Mick Jagger on the classic "Satisfaction" at Madison Square Garden.

"Our music should go anywhere," Stevie said, "as far as the mind can go."

Rock critic Clayton Riley reviewed *Innervisions* on October 21, 1973, in the *New York Times.* His article reflects the recognition that something in Stevie's music reaches beyond the pleasing pop melodies. Stevie was making a place for himself in the struggle to give young black Americans a political, as well as a musical, voice:

> The cut called "He's Mistra Know-It-All" bears solid witness [that] Stevie must *feel* the political climate around him when he sings: "He's a man/With a plan/Got a counterfeit *dollar* in hand . . ." How now, Richard Nixon? . . .
>
> With his facile rhythmic designs, very physical senses of time, the brother *swings,* that is to say he possesses a quality in his work for which the English language provides no more specific definition. (You swing or you don't. Stevie does.)
>
> Like "Living in the City." All waves, you know? Heartbeats and the pulse of an aging dilemma: Black, rural youth wants to find a better place ("A boy is born in hard time Mississippi . . .") and discovers nothing but the city (". . . get in that cell, nigger."). . . . Stevie's enormous visual strength lets him see nearly all the world.

The times were politically charged and Stevie was politically aware. His vignettes, Riley remarks, help us to "see" things. In "Don't You Worry 'bout a Thing," Stevie "worries the tired language to death" in a story about a young black man trying to impress a young woman with lines like "I been, uh, Par-is, Pahru, you know, I mean, I-rock, I-ran . . . Eurasia!"

Known as an innovator in the studio, Stevie brought the same creativity to the promotional trail. In July of 1973, Stevie traveled to New York City to promote the release of *Innervisions.* A bus was reserved in Times Square for the journalists covering the release of his album. Before boarding the bus, all of the journalists were blindfolded;

then they were driven by a confusing route to a location that had been kept secret from them. Stevie had planned a new way of experiencing hearing for his guests, a way to know, for a little while, something that he had always known—what it's like to be blind. "When you look at something, your hearing is distracted by your eye," he would explain afterward.

When they arrived at a nearby recording studio, still blindfolded, an individual guide was waiting for each journalist. The journalists were offered different foods, they examined musical instruments with their hands, and they danced, still blindfolded, to Stevie's new album. This "sensual preview," as Stevie's publicity person called it, was meant to give this small audience an idea of Stevie's inner world, a world without sight that is nonetheless rich in other sensual perceptions. *"Innervisions* gives my own perspective of what's happening in my world, to my people, to all people," Stevie told a journalist. "That's why it took me seven months to get together—I did all the lyrics—and that's why I think it is my most personal album. I don't care if it sells only five copies—this is the way I feel."

The following month brought the nearly tragic accident in North Carolina. Stevie's remarkable comeback was capped off when he took home three 1974 Grammy Awards: Album of the Year, for *Innervisions;* Best Pop Vocal Performance by a Male Singer; and Best Rhythm and Blues Single. By the end of the year Stevie had 14 gold singles (over 1 million sold), four gold albums (500,000 sold), and two platinum albums (over 1 million sold).

Village Voice critic Robert Christgau responded to what many have called the spirituality in Stevie's song lyrics, a quality that listeners have found either inspiring or simple-minded. Calling his fans "Stevie's peace corps," the critic observed that "[s]ometimes the man's success is enough to make you believe in faith." In the song "Visions," Stevie sings, "I'm not the one who make-believes/I know that

En route to the UCLA Medical Center, Lula Hardaway accompanies her famous son through the Los Angeles International Airport, August 20, 1973. Stevie's face shows signs of the serious injuries he sustained two weeks earlier in an automobile accident.

leaves are green/They only turn to brown when autumn comes around." Christgau admitted,

I found myself moved by the "vision in my mind" idea, for obviously the man could enjoy no other, and suddenly I understood how he knew the color of the leaves—he had been told that it was so, and he had no choice but to believe. That was the definitive condition of his life. Much more than you or me, he was in contact with the unconscious acts of faith that get every one of us through each day. . . . [H]e creates an aural universe— or maybe I should call it an aural condition—so rich that it makes us believe. His multiplicity of voices, his heavenly tunes, his wild ear humor, and even his integration of the synthesizer all speak of a free future not dreamt of in our philosophy.

As much as his music and lyrics express his ideas in terms of what we can see, Stevie Wonder's vision is truly an inner vision.

In December, Stevie played the final concert of a 38-city tour that ended where it had begun, at Madison Square Garden. He played for two and a half hours and moved one critic to expound, "[H]e was fantastic, dynamite, terrific, out-of-sight and all those other subjective adjectives that shouldn't be used at all. . . . I mean, he can even get away with a Christmas tree on stage!" Ira Tucker, Stevie's friend and publicist, said, "He knows who he is and where he is," and, quoting from one of Stevie's songs: "It's just been a case of 'Keep on trying, 'til I reach that higher ground.'" At age 24, Stevie Wonder was still climbing to even higher personal and professional ground.

The studio became a haven for the young superstar, who had a knack for creating innovative sounds.

5

IN THE STUDIO

THE TOUR AND the accident behind him, Stevie returned to the process of creating music. At his New York City studio, and later at Wonderland Studios in Los Angeles, Stevie began to draw upon and develop innovative production and sound techniques using the most modern equipment available.

Fulfillingness' First Finale, his next album, was released in July 1974. It rose to the top of the charts with astonishing speed. The most amazing thing about Stevie Wonder, one reviewer wrote, "is that he creates so much of his music on the synthesizer, which he uses as a totally natural extension of himself rather than a dazzling electronic gadget." The album's "triumph of simplicity and warmth" nonetheless points to the struggles and frustrations of life in what is called "the inner-city." The synthesizer and computer techniques Stevie was honing were the most innovative in the music industry; he was able to make them do just about anything he wanted.

But Stevie had a problem that had nothing—and everything—to

51

do with his music: people pretending to be friends merely to be near a rich celebrity. "The bad and the beautiful," wrote a *Newsweek* reporter, "bedevil Stevie more than most celebrities—his charisma draws hangers-on and his blindness makes him more vulnerable. . . . Much of his life (when Stevie is not on tour) is now centered in a super-equipped sixteen-track recording studio in Los Angeles, which has quickly become a mecca for musicians, groupies and even superstars who are eager to do business with Stevie." For the young genius, a crisis was brewing in the form of an ever-growing number of "drones," as recording engineer Robert Margoulef called them, who would "pull him down and isolate him from the very things that made him good." Luckily, the people closest to Stevie were there to help him. "Stevie's area of genius is music, and, in the other areas, although he's very competent, he's still only 24," Malcolm Cecil said at the time. "He has to deal with many levels of his reality through the eyes and trust of many other people."

It's true that lots of people wanted to work with or simply be near Stevie in the hopes that his genius and charisma might be contagious or that his money would flow freely. But not all of these associations were parasitic. On *Fulfillingness,* the Jackson 5, Minne Riperton, and Paul Anka lent their voices to produce the rich harmonies to Stevie's instrumentals. Those who worked with him to produce his albums were both loyal and protective of Stevie.

The albums Stevie recorded during the 1970s were made in technical collaboration with synthesizer technicians and recording engineers Margoulef and Cecil. They would operate the technical "boards" while Stevie controlled the keyboards and the style of the effects. With his electronic tools, he explored and experimented with every new sound he could. The electronic "bag of tricks" they had assembled included an effect that music critics and journalists could not figure out. Margoulef and Cecil called it Stevie's "bag voice sound." Margoulef eventually solved the mystery of the technological wonder: To produce the effect, a loudspeaker driver was placed inside a cloth bag that had a hose attached to one end. Stevie would run a synthesized sound through the speaker, place one end of the hose into his mouth, and enunciate the lyrics to the song he was working on. The result was appropriately named the "bag voice sound."

When asked whether or not this might have been the craziest musical instrument setup they'd ever worked with, Margoulef replied, "They were *all* crazy." From the African talking drum used with bells on the song "Big Brother," to the Clavinet, a 5-octave electronic instrument similar to an electric piano, Stevie used every sound-making tool available. What he always found most exciting, however, was the Moog synthesizer, which he said enabled him to "create various sounds, bass sounds" and to "bend notes the way I [hear] them." Stevie's goal is never to merely create a novelty, but somehow to catch for recording the sounds he already hears in the world.

In October 1976, after signing a $13 million contract with Motown, Stevie released the double album *Songs in the Key of Life,* which was viewed by critics as his most ambitious work to date. Fans took to the album as well, making it his most commercially successful album to that point. It was only the third album in history to land immediately in the number one spot on the Billboard charts— and it remained at the top of the charts for 14 weeks. Stevie showed that he had mastered a variety of musical forms, techniques, and instruments. On the album he included the fusion-jazz tune "Contusion" (possibly a wry personal salute to the contusions suffered in the accident), the gospel-soul song "As," the funky "I Wish," the joyful tribute to Duke Ellington, "Sir Duke," and another to his newborn daughter, "Isn't She Lovely." *Songs in the Key of Life* confirmed Stevie's status as one of the most admired

Stevie's image towers over Times Square in New York City after the release of Songs in the Key of Life. *The 1976 masterpiece debuted at the top of the charts and stayed there for 14 weeks.*

contemporary musicians and songwriters. Nearly 20 years later, rapper Coolio would cover a song from the album, "Pastime Paradise," arranging, singing, and renaming it "Gangsta Paradise."

To everyone's surprise, Stevie didn't release any new recordings for three years after *Songs in the Key of Life.* He took time off to devote his energies to a new kind of project, the soundtrack music for a documentary film, *Journey Through the Secret Life of Plants.* When the double album was released in 1979, however, reviews and sales were disappointing. Although the project has since come to be seen as a landmark of instrumental and songwriting achievement and a precursor to New Age music, at the time *Village Voice* critic Stephen Holden called it "a vision as achingly sweet as it is profoundly foolish." In December, Stevie performed the score at New York's Metropolitan Opera House with Wonderlove and the National Afro-American Philharmonic Orchestra. A reviewer called the performance "great American music" with "a sweeping grandeur."

The documentary film was never released, but this symphonic suite of songs would remain one of Stevie's personal favorites, a work of which he has always been proud. He has said that one of the most powerful influences upon his work was the Japanese keyboardist Isao Tomita. The synthesized adaptations Tomita performs of the music of Debussy, Mussorgsky, and Stravinsky drew Stevie to late romantic music and to many of the themes he explored in his own album.

Stevie hugs Coretta Scott King as they celebrate the signing of a bill making the birthday of Coretta's husband, slain civil rights leader Dr. Martin Luther King Jr., a national holiday. The 1980s saw Stevie take an active role in numerous causes, including the push for a holiday honoring King.

6

TAKING IT
ON THE ROAD

BY THE 1980S, Stevie's studio work was taking a backseat to his touring. By the end of the decade he would be the first Motown artist to play in the Eastern bloc (European communist countries under the influence of the former Soviet Union).

In the early part of the decade Stevie lent his talent, time, and celebrity to many causes that were not the headline grabbers most artists of his stature would seek out: He worked on behalf of the family of Eula Love, a black woman killed in a controversial confrontation with Los Angeles police. He performed at a high school rally for Students Against Drunk Driving, and he appeared with Jackson Browne in what was called the "Peace Rally" at the Rose Bowl. Later, he and fellow artists would work together on behalf of many worldwide charities.

Modern technology had become part of every aspect of Stevie's work, from brainstorming in a hotel room to arena sound production. He had become a one-man band whenever and wherever he traveled.

With a Yamaha DX7 synthesizer, a Linn drum machine, and a small, portable speaker system, he worked on pieces in his hotel room while he was on the road. This was perhaps Stevie's most commercially successful decade, and he continued to pour unbounded energy into his music, but critics were not enthusiastic about his work. They felt that he was not living up to the excellence they had come to expect from him.

If his critics were disappointed with his work in the 1980s, this did not keep fans away from Stevie's albums or live concerts. During his six nights performing at London's Wembley Arena in September 1980, he drew 60,000 people. After one show, a two-and-a-half-hour marathon, critic Derek Jewell asked, "What can't he do within his chosen ground? He swings, he is blues, he is jazz, he is street life ('Living in the City,' brilliant), he uplifts and thinks and rarely, even when naïve, fails to sound convincing." Stevie's showmanship is as important as his compositions. Onstage, he is what Clayton Riley called "The Wonder."

Later that year Stevie again played at Madison Square Garden. Gil Scott-Heron and reggae star Bob Marley opened the show. Both Scott-Heron and Marley were known for the political and social awareness represented in their songs, and Stevie wanted to include their emotionally charged work in his show. But the seriousness of the message always gives way to the music when Stevie is onstage. Robert Palmer wrote in the *New York Times* of one of the Garden shows, "Again and again, Mr. Wonder would sing the first line of one of his songs, bask in the audience's shouts of recognition, hurry through a truncated version of the song, and move along to another one. He would build intimate moods only to shatter them with pointless vocal grandstanding. It was his sheer presence that was most important; the music was a significant, but secondary, concern." The best quality of a live performance sometimes consists of the very imperfection of it—the unplanned moments, the surprises, the attraction of the unexpected. Stevie's onstage restlessness at the Garden that night prompted criticism, but the high points stood out even more.

Stevie released a new album, *Hotter Than July,* in September 1980. The album included a song for the slain civil rights leader Dr. Martin Luther King Jr., "Happy Birthday," as well as a song many fans consider a classic, "Masterblaster (Jamming)." Stevie's critics and fans thought he was back on track, but the failure of the *Secret Life of Plants* film project had made him cautious. Delays and postponements became common in his recording process.

His caution did not, however, prevent him from participating in events to support various causes. The song for Dr. King called for a national holiday for the civil rights leader. Stevie put his career on hold for almost two years in order to achieve this goal. He marched, spoke at rallies, and gave interviews, and "Happy Birthday" became the unofficial theme song of the movement. At last, on January 15, 1986, President Ronald Reagan declared Dr. Martin Luther King Jr.'s birthday a national holiday. When Arizona decided not to join the rest of the country in recognizing the day, Stevie called for a boycott of the entire state. The Arizona government soon reversed its stance. The first Martin Luther King Day was celebrated with a concert at which Stevie Wonder topped the bill, and "Happy Birthday" continues to be played on many radio stations to mark King's birthday, officially celebrated on the third Monday in January.

The 1980s also saw Stevie collaborate on songs for other artists' albums. In 1982 he recorded two duets with Paul McCartney, "Ebony and Ivory" and "What's That You're Doing?" for McCartney's album *Tug of War.* In 1985 a duet with Michael Jackson, "Just Good Friends," appeared on Jackson's album *Bad,* and "My Love," a duet with Julio Iglesias, was released on Igelsias's 1988

Stevie performs with Wonder-love at "Peace Sunday," a nuclear disarmament rally. The event was held June 7, 1982, in the Rose Bowl in Pasadena, California.

album *Non Stop.* Stevie also played harmonica on Elton John's "I Guess That's Why They Call It the Blues." Stevie had been featured with various artists on many albums throughout the '60s and '70s, but almost all had been under the auspices and control of Motown. In the 1980s he moved from the Motown sound to a broader-based musical style.

In 1982, he released a retrospective double album, *Stevie Wonder's Original Musiquarium I.* It included four new recordings and what critics thought was his best work since 1971. But Stevie decided not to release his next album, *People Move, Human Plays.* Instead, he accepted Gene Wilder's request to compose the soundtrack music for his upcoming film *The Woman in Red.* On this album he used the Kurzweil 250 synthesizer and the Synclavier keyboard to sample and reproduce the musical sounds that were threaded throughout the songs.

In 1985 one song from *The Woman in Red,* the ballad "I Just Called to Say I Love You," won an Oscar for Best Original Song. Stevie accepted the Oscar in the name of Nelson Mandela, the black South African civil rights leader and Johannesburg lawyer. Mandela had been sentenced to life in prison in 1964 on charges that he had conspired to overthrow the government. The South African government's apartheid policies, which segregated blacks and other races from whites, brought contempt and trade bans from the United States and other nations. In retaliation for Stevie's political action, the South African government banned Stevie's music in the country. "If my being banned means people will be free, ban me megatimes!" he said in response. The same year, Stevie was arrested with other antiapartheid demonstrators for marching too close to the South African embassy in Washington, D.C. Eventually, Mandela would be freed as apartheid disintegrated. The voice of Stevie Wonder, along with many others, made the world aware of the need for things to change, for everyone to speak up and call attention to the world's injustices.

The success of "I Just Called to Say I Love You," a lightweight composition both musically and conceptually, surprised Stevie and Motown. This and other songs like "Part-Time Lover" and "Overjoyed" convinced many that Stevie was writing beneath his capabilities. However, the simple melodies and words of songs such as "Heaven

Help Us All," "Isn't She Lovely," and "As" have made them internationally appealing and memorable.

In October 1983 Stevie performed eight concerts at Radio City Music Hall in New York. At the time Stephen Holden remarked that Stevie had "emerged as something of a spiritual leader, singing and talking peace and interracial love and of a humanist philosophy that he calls L.L.M.O., which stands for Letting Life Move On." Stevie's sense of humor was also on display at the Radio City concerts, as Holden observed: "Looking back at his early Motown days, when his voice began to change, [he] used a voice filter that pitched his baritone an octave higher. [Comedian] Eddie Murphy, who is noted for his amusing parody of [Stevie], also appeared, and the two engaged in affectionate banter." As in all of his concerts, he engaged the audience and "conjured a spirit of love" to which even the most reserved of critics never failed to respond.

Despite his numerous accolades as a musical artist, Stevie wanted to do more than merely entertain with his songs. After he was presented the key to the city of Detroit, Stevie wondered whether politics, perhaps as mayor of Detroit, might be a useful way to direct his energies. But he could not abandon performing just yet; his music gave him a more direct way to talk to people than politics could offer.

In March 1985, We Are the World (also called United Support of Artists for Africa), with its now well-known theme song of the same name, was assembled to aid the organization USA for Africa. Stevie was the second of 21 soloists on the record, which also included Bob Dylan, Ray Charles, Harry Belafonte, Bruce Springsteen, Lionel Richie, Michael Jackson, the Pointer Sisters, and Tina Turner. The same year, he helped record an album to support AmFAR (American Foundation for AIDS Research); on *Dionne & Friends: That's What Friends Are For,* Stevie joined artistic forces with, among others,

Dionne Warwick, Elton John, Gladys Knight, and Quincy Jones. His performance on Warwick's title song became another hit for Stevie. In 1989 Stevie traveled to Poland to sing a benefit concert at the offices of the Polish labor union Solidarity. Later that year he participated in a global telecast called *Our Common Future,* a program meant to educate the world about the deterioration of the environment. He also contributed a song to an album to benefit a Romanian relief drive.

USA for Africa gathered on January 28, 1985, to record the historic "We Are the World." Pictured (clockwise from left) are Lionel Richie, Daryl Hall, Quincy Jones, Paul Simon, and Stevie Wonder.

Stevie is arrested near the South African embassy in Washington, D.C., February 14, 1985. He and a group of demonstrators were protesting South Africa's policy of apartheid.

The persistence of racism in America and apartheid in South Africa, violence in the inner cities, drunk driving, drug abuse, homelessness, and hunger in Ethiopia were among the world and community issues that troubled him. He wanted to make a difference. But to make a difference, his music had to come first. On the road for charity causes or for concerts, Stevie never seemed to take a break; he was always preparing new material, no matter where he was.

One reporter met with Stevie for an interview in the star's hotel room after a concert. The reporter described being treated to an impromptu performance of songs Stevie was working on for his next album, the long-awaited *In Square Circle:* "Even in these spare, off-the-cuff versions, the new songs showed the composer's passionate, tumbling chromaticism reaching new peaks of refinement. Backing himself with a drum machine, he also turned to a grand piano and began improvising jazz in short, percussive phrases whose rich harmonies were a natural extension of his songwriting style."

In Square Circle, released in 1985, marked a return to the melodic music Stevie had written and sung during the 1970s. "Part-Time Lover," a single from the album, became the first single to simultaneously top the *Billboard* pop, R & B, adult contemporary, and dance/disco charts. The album reached number five on the charts and won Stevie a Grammy for Best R & B Vocal Performance. Along with light ballads, such as "Stranger on the Shore of Love," Stevie included songs of social protest on this album.

Stevie Wonder was now looked upon as one of the elder statesmen of black music and a champion of African-American causes. "I knew that [changing musical direction] was risky," Stevie told an interviewer about the more serious tone of many of his lyrics on *In Square Circle,* "but I didn't really think of that as being a reason I should stop. I thought it was more important for me to express those things, to deal with those topics that were not only on my mind but heavy on my heart. . . . [T]hese were and are issues we need to deal with, that need to be confronted."

Stevie's "Wonder in Square Circle" tour played eight shows at New York's Madison Square Garden. The shows lasted three and a half hours, and the production was spectacular. Stevie played on an in-the-round stage on a drifting platform that enabled him to play to each corner of the cavernous auditorium. For those too far from the stage to see everything, a multicamera audio-video system provided views of the action on huge screens, along with video clips and quadraphonic sound. "Did Stevie Wonder *need* this kind of production?" asked a reviewer. "No—he deserved it." The crowd responded with enthusiasm and emotion, rising to its feet for "Masterblaster" and a medley of "Signed, Sealed, Delivered (I'm Yours)," "Uptight," and "I Was Made to Love Her." Stevie's rendition of the Isley Brothers' famous oldie "Shout" created what one fan called "the first real moments of pandemonium." And Stevie moved his audience in a different way with Dylan's "Blowin' in the Wind," making his keyboard sound like a guitar. But he saved his most serious song for the end. In "It's Wrong," a song against apartheid, Stevie, accompanied by an African chorus, sang: "You know apartheid's wrong, wrong /Like slavery was wrong, wrong / Like the Holocaust was wrong, wrong." The forceful battle cry ended with a vow: "Freedom is coming/ Hold on tight."

A reviewer called the show "a meaningful display of a greatly gifted man's craft, concern, and humanity." Another reviewer wrote, "Only Stevie Wonder is a one-man band with the range of an orchestra whose moral stature transcends the pop realm. Stevie Wonder at 34 is almost a force of nature." Stevie has described his stance toward the world and the place of his music perhaps better than anyone else can: "Life, there's always the same things going on. There's always a fire burning somewhere, there's always people falling in love, there's always people fighting in the world. My music reflects all of that."

Whatever their concerns, whatever their circumstances, Stevie's audience never fails to respond to his music—and to his onstage charisma. In August 1988,

Stevie's show, "Wonder Summer of Fun" played eight nights at New York's Radio City Music Hall. One reviewer observed, "Wonder's show integrated new songs with a large portion of the soundtrack of our lives—amazingly written and sung by just one man."

Stevie hugs South African president Nelson Mandela, February 1996. Through his music, his public performances, and private actions, Stevie had long supported Mandela in his fight against apartheid.

7

FIGHTING THE GOOD FIGHT

BY HIS 30TH birthday, Stevie Wonder had been a singer, songwriter, and musician for almost 19 years. With 21 gold singles, five platinum albums, and nine Grammy Awards, he was voted into the Songwriters Hall of Fame in 1982. In addition to the wide recognition and respect for his artistry, Stevie had become world renowned for his devotion to social causes. He wanted to change the world. "Wherever people were striving," writer Leonard Pitts Jr. observed, "he was there. Whether the issue was police brutality, hunger, human rights or the environment, Stevie was a tireless campaigner for justice." He was no longer the naive and sheltered prodigy. He had worked with the best musicians and performers in music; he had become a father, a shrewd businessman controlling a multimillion-dollar business that employed 100 people, and an active humanitarian.

During the 1980s Stevie began to speak out as a Christian, in the tradition of Dr. King, on behalf of nonviolent action for human rights. In May 1985 he addressed the United Nations General Assembly in protest against South African apartheid: "No one, of any color or culture," he

Stevie gives an impromptu performance for delegates to the United Nations, which had honored him for his work against apartheid, May 13, 1985. It was his 35th birthday.

said, "has any covenant with God that says he, she or they are better than anyone because of the color of their skin."

Although determined to bring to public attention many important issues, especially racism, Stevie never lets rage or obscenity color his songs. He has actually received plenty of criticism from current rap and hip-hop stars for this lack of rage in his lyrics. In an interview with the *Toronto Star,* he explained, "I think that you cannot really be the best if you're going to let anger be the thing that controls you more than what you have to say." In another interview, he expressed concern that pop artists were not exercising enough thoughtful control over their own work, that brutality and expressions of hate in lyrics may affect young listeners. "The more people are allowed to be frank in their music—brutally frank and graphic about sex, death, violence, whatever the current trend happens to be—the more people will be hearing some things not meant to be taken literally," he says. "We can't honestly say that gangsta rap has never driven an impressionable kid to wanna 'walk that walk.'"

Stevie believed that being a popular musician and songwriter should be something more than what it had become for many musicians: "It's not about getting a message across anymore—it's all [about] how much money can be generated. . . . People don't want the truth, they want the juice, the gossip. We're more comfortable looking at people and judging them than we are taking a long, hard look at ourselves. I'm always hearing people say, 'Wow, this world is really messed up'—as if they don't live in it." In contrast, he had finally reached a position from which he could make a difference, and he intended to wield all the influence he had amassed in order to do so.

In *Ebony* magazine, writer Jack Slater described the place Stevie had come to occupy both professionally and personally and the growing power his reputation brought:

> [He] has grown from cute child prodigy into one of this country's most respected artists: a veritable national treasure. That kind of success equals power, power that can keep planes and television shows and awards dinners—and people—waiting. Power which is tolerated because it is so friendly; power which is seductive because it seems so unpretentious.
>
> "Nobody can ever be angry with Steve for long," said the young man who knows his boss. "He's just too damned nice."
>
> Stevie Wonder is, in fact, very much like his music: warm, romantic, spiritual, political. . . . [He] subscribes to the belief that "all living things are bound together by one consciousness."

Any performer referred to as a "national treasure" may also be a magnet for gossip and unwelcome scrutiny. Stories about rock and roll stars with big talent and small personal character don't surprise the public very much anymore. But

Stevie Wonder, "too damn nice" to be angry with, has a combination of talent, power, and character that rarely seems to coexist comfortably in any one person.

Characters, released in November 1987, offers a gritty take on politics in the 1980s. The songs on this album mark Stevie's commitment to change the political and social world with his gift: his songs. "Skeletons," released as a single, uses actual voices from the news, including those of President Ronald Reagan and Lieutenant Colonel Oliver North, the military official at the heart of the infamous Iran-Contra scandal. (The U.S. government was found to have secretly sold arms to Iran and to have given the proceeds to Nicaraguan rebels.) Stevie's responses are part of the song: "stinkin' lies," he sneers. "Dark 'n' Lovely" is yet another meditative ballad about South African apartheid. Other songs on the album are vignettes, stories about people in terrifying or pivotal situations demanding that choices be made. "You Will Know," the album's opening song, is a ballad about a drug user and a struggling single parent; on "In Your Corner," Stevie plays the part of a bad companion who tries to manipulate a friend into illegal behavior. "Get It" is a spirited duet with Michael Jackson, and "Come Let Me Make Your Love Come Down" features a synthesized, blues-style big band, with guitar solos from B. B. King and Stevie Ray Vaughan.

In January 1989, at age 38, Stevie accepted a distinct honor. He became one of the youngest artists ever inducted into the Rock 'n' Roll Hall of Fame.

Despite his fame, however, Stevie zealously guards his private life, having seen other artists consumed by the spotlight. Family still seems to play an important role. His children, mother, brothers, sister, and longtime friends will always remain at the heart of Stevie's world. They protect him from hangers-on, and he, in turn, includes them in all aspects of his musical life, from songwriting to the nuts and bolts of stage production.

In the early 1990s, Stevie was urged by many to run for mayor of Detroit. This time he carefully considered the

Worldwide appeal: Patients of the National Rehabilitation Centre for the Handicapped in Taounda, Cameroon, surround the American music superstar Stevie Wonder during a visit he made to the African nation in July 1992.

possibility, but once again he decided against a life in politics, believing that his work as an entertainer allowed him to reach more people and accomplish more good. Through his music he had won a forum to speak about whatever concerned him. Now that he had the complete artistic control he had worked so hard to secure, public office would be too confining. Other venues for social action were open to a singer and songwriter whose name and work were recognized by millions of people all over the world.

In 1993 Stevie participated in a major concert tour for the Charge Against Hunger, an international food aid campaign sponsored by American Express and Share Our Strength, a nonprofit relief organization. During the Christmas holidays he also visited many American schools to speak about the need to help the hungry. "If I could use anything that I have been given by God to help other people, you know, I'm down with that," he told a reporter covering the events. In November, he sang "Take Time Out," a song he had written for the campaign against hunger, at the Macy's Thanksgiving Day parade in New York City.

On his next album, *Conversation Peace,* released in March 1995, Stevie continued to focus on the message of world peace. The title itself is part of his message in two ways: as a call for dialogue among individuals and communities, both at home and abroad; and as a reminder that conversation between neighbors and nations may be able to create peace among them. Our words matter, he tells us. Stevie had first titled the album "Conversation Piece," but changed it after hearing many people using the word *peace* in their conversations. He began to wonder if people even thought about what they were saying. "Words have a lot of power," said Stevie, "so when you say it from your mouth it's got to mean more than you just saying it." He played London's Royal Albert Hall to promote *Conversation Peace* and scheduled two additional charity concerts there.

To no one's surprise, Stevie was a prominent participant in the 1995 Million Man March in Washington, D.C. Stevie joined the likes of Maya Angelou, Jesse Jackson, Betty Shabazz (the widow of Malcom X), Rosa Parks, and Louis Farrakhan as speakers at the event, held to celebrate ideas of family and parenting valued by all Americans and, particularly, the African-American husband and dad. Stevie was there as a celebrity and as a member of the African-American community— especially as a dad. High school students Milton Boy and Bashure Wilson along with 10-year-old Tiffany

Stevie addresses participants in the Million Man March, October 16, 1995.

Mayo recited poems with Stevie before the hundreds of thousands of men assembled. Stevie said,

> I cannot visually see you but I can your spirits, and I can feel your presence. . . . I'm here for every poor man born in the ghetto, every middle class [man] born in the middle class, and for every rich man, to say that no matter where we might be in class, we are all one people.
>
> Staring right at 2000 A.D., as if mankind's atrocities to man [have] no history, but [in] just a glance at life in 2000 B.C. we find traces of man's inhumanity to man. There goes history. All for one, one for all. There's no way unless we heed the call. Me for you, you for me. There's no chance of world salvation unless the conversation speaks.

Over the years, Stevie's interest in social issues

expanded to the continent of Africa. The poverty, disease, famine, and economic peril in which sub-Saharan countries find themselves led to a campaign in June 2000 called the Jubilee 2000 Debt Relief Campaign. American churches and other organizations worldwide challenged rich nations to cancel the debilitating debt owed to them by these impoverished countries. The debt, according to the World Bank, amounts to nearly $400 for every man, woman, and child in sub-Saharan Africa.

To fully understand the burden such a debt imposes, consider Mozambique as an example. In that country, one of every four children dies before age five as a result of infectious disease. Yet the government spends four times more on debt than on health care. The pope, the Dalai Lama, Bishop Desmond Tutu, Muhammad Ali, United Nations Secretary General Kofi Annan, Reverend Jesse Jackson, Sir Anthony Hopkins, singers Bono and Lauryn Hill, and Stevie Wonder joined thousands more to call attention to this crisis and to the opportunity for the world to alleviate suffering on a huge scale. In the end the debts weren't canceled, but the campaign made the world aware of the problem and changed the way in which at least some of this debt will be structured. In the company of the world's most powerful voices of conscience, Stevie helped to offer a fresh and urgent perspective on African issues. And Stevie, like the most noteworthy men and women of conscience, is patient and persistent, willing to campaign again and again to accomplish change. He continues to ask us, in his music and by his example, to examine ourselves and our responsibilities as citizens of the world.

Tireless as he is in the service of social change, Stevie's strongest vehicle for his message continues to be his music. During his concerts he has always taken a moment to remind his audience that something to strive for is "pure love between all people, a love that is willing to give honestly and sincerely regardless of the color of your skin." Unfortunately, Stevie adds, "the only place where I find this love that I talk about is in my dreams, in the songs that I write."

Stevie's 1995 live album *Natural Wonder* once again showed his innovative approach to music and his willingness to experiment with new musical ideas. The album includes many old Stevie Wonder favorites rearranged for a 30-piece symphony orchestra. It would certainly have been easier for Stevie to play them as he always had, using the multitracking techniques he had perfected, but he wanted to try something different. *Stevie Wonder at the Close of the Century,* a four-CD compilation of the best works of his career, released in 1999, is a musical gift drawn from four decades of the development of a cultural icon.

In its January 2000 "Millennium Special," *Rolling Stone* magazine asked many of the most accomplished actors, writers, and musicians what they thought were the most important political and social events of the past century. Stevie named the end of apartheid in South Africa and the tearing down of the Berlin Wall, which marked the fall of communism. "We have come far," he acknowledged, "but it can happen again. As crazy as humans are, it can all happen again." When asked who he would consider his heroes, Stevie observed, "There are two people who stirred a kind of emotion for me like no other: Martin Luther King, Jr., and John Lennon. For years after Lennon was killed, I could not hear [his song] 'Imagine' without crying. . . . [I]t only takes one person not to understand."

Throughout his musical career Stevie has been known as an innovator, and he brings that same spirit to other areas of his life. Here he and SAP chief executive officer Paul Wahl (right) examine a Braille reader for the Internet. The device was a contender for the 1998 SAP/Stevie Wonder Vision Awards, which are given for products, people, and organizations that aid the blind and visually impaired.

8

A BRIGHT
FUTURE

AS A MAJOR figure in pop music in the 1970s, Stevie was followed
everywhere by reporters and interviewers trying to capture everything he said. He attempted to satisfy some of this curiosity by
giving interviews in which he tried to explain the mechanics of his
creative process. "I guess it might seem odd to you," he told one
interviewer, "but the way I think about making my music, I think
it's very visual." He described how he surrounded himself with
electronic devices that "remember every melody" he might whistle
or hum. "With the help of these things," said Stevie, "I have a
much greater ability to get any sound I can hear in my head out
into a memory bank or on a keyboard. It gives me the chance to
really express my ideas—and for a blind person, especially, this
just opens up possibilities that even 10 years ago we could hardly
have imagined."

In 1974, when asked what he would like to see, Stevie
replied, as he usually does, the world, the earth, the birds, the

grass, and the people he loves. "But there are a lot of things I wouldn't want to see," he said. "Destruction, corruption and war. Hate and sin. But you can already feel all those things anyway. It may sound contradictory, but if I did see such ugly things, they would make me appreciate the beauty I already know even more."

Stevie's songs, filled with allusions to seeing the world, reveal his ability to describe the things he has never actually seen. In "Paul's Perspective" he writes: "Look at the sun, feel its rays / with such a smiling face maybe we can't, but maybe we can / share it with all the world." The song "Another Star" states: "For you there might be a brighter star / but through my eyes the light of you is all I see." At times he talks naturally in visual metaphors, and he has always had a unique sort of vision. But if the world of vision for Stevie Wonder is a matter of belief—an "unconscious act of faith"—and an inspiration for music, it is also a purely practical matter, for a blind artist as much as for, perhaps, a sighted airline attendant, as he tells it: "[A] stewardess will come up and say . . . 'Here's your fork, you can eat now.' I'm not helpless. I don't want the white cane. I don't need the guide dog. I want to be independent!"

An important way Stevie has made himself independent is through the use of computer and electronic technology—not just for making music, but to accomplish and experience things most of us take for granted. For instance, Stevie takes notes on a computer that prints them out in Braille. He listens to recorded books. He plays tennis with balls that emit a beep.

But his most astonishing experience had nothing to do with computers—or sight. He attended the births of two of his three children. "I felt them being born—it was amazing," he recalls.

In 1995 he combined his love of children and his

desire to illuminate the world of the blind. Through words, music, sounds, and Braille, Stevie wrote a storybook for children called *Little Stevie Wonder in Places Under the Sun.* It tells a story about Stevie's travels to Japan with two friends. A Braille translation of the text appears on each page, with a complete Braille alphabet for sighted children to learn. Stevie's son, Mumtaz, was chosen to be the voice of Stevie in the recording of the book.

In May 1997 the first SAP/Stevie Wonder Vision Awards were held in Los Angeles at a publicity event dubbed the Surprise Birthday Party for Stevie Wonder. SAP (Systems, Applications, and Products in Data Processing), Inc., operates all over the world to develop information technology to enable the blind and people with other disabilities to fully use their skills and talents. Stevie's commitment to SAP was personal as well as public:

> People will hear and they will be encouraged to help someone they know who has a disability—maybe a cousin or a friend. They will have a greater desire to see that person be more independent . . . and better determine his or her own destiny. This is a people thing; this is a life thing. . . . I do believe that we, as human beings, are channels that can be used for great things.

SAP collaborated with Stevie in recognizing a product, a person, and an organization that had developed a way to bring the blind and visually impaired into the workplace. They offered a total of $500,000 in cash prizes as both a reward for extraordinary accomplishments that enhance the lives of people with disabilities and an impetus to further research and development. The theme of the birthday party was acknowledging that everyone is an individual, as well as a member of the world community—and that every person has something to offer others. The product that won the SAP/Stevie Wonder Vision Award, and which Stevie uses, is the Kurzweil 1000, a PC-based

Stevie shows off his book, Little Stevie Wonder in Places Under the Sun, *at the 1996 Helen Keller Achievement Awards.*

reading system for the blind that converts printed words into speech through scanning technology known as optical character recognition (OCR). Stevie was proud to be involved with the ceremony, but he joked that he had a secret personal wish for the SAP/Stevie Wonder Vision Awards: "The real reason that I got involved in this whole thing was because, I figure, about two years from now, I'd like to be driving!"

Though driving may be out of the question, it seemed for a brief time that technology might actually allow him to see. In November 1999, Stevie stunned a congregation in a Detroit church by announcing that he was going to undergo tests to determine whether or not he would be a candidate to receive a retinal implant that could give him some vision. The technology has been in development at Johns Hopkins University's Wilmer Eye Institute for a decade. The system electronically transmits images to the brain to create vision by means of a camera mounted on a pair of glasses and a computer chip—an intraocular retinal prosthesis—surgically implanted in the back of the eye. The camera transmits the image to the computer chip, which is connected to tissue in the back of the eye (the retina). The inventor of this "retinal microchip," Wentai Liu, describes the challenge of developing such a device: "Our biggest challenge is to learn how to encase the chip so it can be implanted in the eye. Fluids in the eye have to be kept outside the chip, and the chip has to be kept from further damaging the retina, which has been likened in its delicacy to wet tissue paper."

The vision that is promised by such a computer chip is uncertain and incomplete by most standards. However, the head of the Hopkins team, Dr. Mark Humayan, is convinced that enough vision may be achieved by this system "to allow a person to walk through a room and maybe recognize a face." That was enough encouragement for Stevie to meet with the doctors to discuss whether or not he might be helped by a retinal microchip implant. Unfortunately for Stevie, researchers now think that the people most likely to be helped by the chip are those who suffer from an inherited condition, retinitis pigmentosa. The best candidates for the implant are people who once had full vision, but research continues, and within three years the implant may be widely available. More research will, perhaps, yield something for Stevie. "I have this idea in my head where a blind person would be able to drive," he told an interviewer in 1986. "I've learned nothing is impossible." Stevie remains optimistic, and a bit philosophical:

> I think that there is God's divine plan and as much as it was a misfortune for me to end up . . . blind, I don't feel that I have missed out on too much in life; there are things that I sometimes think I've seen even more vividly than people that can see, and I think that all of us—whether we see or not—we use a lot of what we hear as our first and sometimes lasting impressions.

But Stevie's dream of vision persists. He had hoped that medical science would find a way, whether with eye transplants or a miniaturized video device attached to the optic nerve, to enable the blind to see. Now his dream no longer seems like science fiction.

In the midst of developing his musical talent and achieving his greatest commercial success during the 1980s, Stevie was already thinking ahead to the time when he would be able to devote more attention to his family and live his life a little less in the public eye. He is a private man, one who, though very open and honest with everyone he talks to, wants his music to stand on its own. Like the author of a book, Stevie writes songs about what he thinks, but the narrator, the voice of the song's speaking character, is a little outside the man who composed it. Whether singing his own songs or those of other artists,

Stevie says his message is in the music:

> I hope in the coming years to do a book about myself.
> . . . But my music actually speaks closer to me than any-
> thing [else] I could ever do. If you listen to the songs I've
> written, or to the songs of others I record, you will hear
> how I feel. I guess it's the deepest me. Sometimes I feel
> that the people who listen to my music, or the fans that I
> have, are closer to me than some of the people who are
> my close acquaintances or friends. And that's why it's so
> important to me to give you all that I'm feeling.

Despite the incredible obstacles he has faced, he continues to send out the most positive of messages in his music.
"In the spirit realm," Stevie told writer Michael Datcher, "we
have the highest of all—God. Music has been here since the
beginning of time, [the] sound of earth itself, birds singing.
From an environmental sense we, being the original people
of the planet, instinctually have a love and appreciation for
music. People say, 'Look into the eyes and you see the
windows of the soul.' You look into music and you see the
spirit." Stevie has always tried to reflect the society we live
in and "yet be optimistic about those things that [are] not
happening." However terrible a situation or an event may be,
we always have a chance to improve things, to perhaps
escape the worst that people can do to each other.

Stevie has been asked about the legacy he hopes to
leave. What will become of the musical genius? How
would he like to be remembered? He has responded:

> Either you live to die or you die living. I will die living.
> I want my legacy to be that everyone I have loved—
> children, wife, family, fans—knows that I was a lover of
> life, that I was so very honored to be on this planet, and
> thankful to be chosen as one of the people that God chose
> to express not only my feelings, but hopefully the feelings
> of many people who never had the chance to do so.

Of course, Stevie isn't quite through creating his

Flanked by his son, Keita, and daughter, Aisha, Stevie accepts a lifetime achievement award at the 38th Annual Grammy Awards in Los Angeles, February 26, 1996.

legacy just yet. He has plans to release both a studio album and a gospel album on the Motown label, where he has spent most of his career. It is a career that has spanned four decades, a career that has already seen him become one of the most popular recording artists in history, surpassed in the production of top 10 hits only by Elvis Presley and the Beatles.

In a professional world where performers leave their recording roots as soon as they become stars, Stevie Wonder is unusual. "I'm a May person," he says, "a Taurus.

I have a place of loyalty and that's important to me. As long as Motown is a place where I can grow musically, I'll be there."

The walls of his Los Angeles studio are covered in African mudcloth, "a visual symbol," Datcher observes, "for a man who sees by feeling." No doubt in his trademark sunglasses, characteristically rocking to the music he seeks, Stevie will continue to find ways to give a musical voice to the sounds he already hears.

CHRONOLOGY

1950   Stevland Judkins born May 13 in Saginaw, Michigan, the third son of Lula Mae Morris Hardaway; becomes blind shortly after birth because of the administering of too much oxygen in a hospital incubator.

1953   The family moves to Detroit and Lula is reunited with the father of Stevie's two older brothers. Stevie joins a church choir; at the same time, he is introduced to the rhythm and blues sound of artists such as Sam Cooke, Ray Charles, B.B. King, Jackie Wilson, the Coasters, and Bobby Bland.

1961   Signs with Motown Records and becomes known as Little Stevie Wonder. To protect the 11-year-old's earnings, Stevie is adopted by his great-uncle Walter Morris and becomes Stevland Morris.

1968   Graduates with high school diploma from Michigan School for the Blind.

1970   Marries Syreeta Wright; she helps him to write many of his songs and develops her own talents as a singer-songwriter.

1971   At 21, negotiates new contract with Motown and gains complete artistic control of his work; forms his own production and publishing companies, Taurus Productions and Black Bull.

1972   Forms his backup group Wonderlove; joins John Lennon and Yoko Ono in concert at Madison Square Garden, New York. Marriage to Wright ends in divorce.

1973   Tours United States with the Rolling Stones. In August, involved in near-fatal car crash while on tour in North Carolina; in a coma for one day; loses sense of smell.

1974   Son Mumtaz born. *Fulfillingness' First Finale* (album) released. *Innervisions* wins three Grammy Awards. Los Angeles proclaims November 22 "Stevie Wonder Day."

1975   *Fulfillingness' First Finale* wins four Grammy Awards; daughter Aisha born, which inspires song "Isn't She Lovely."

1976   Son Keita born.

1982   With Bob Dylan and Jackson Browne, plays at "Peace Sunday" antinuclear rally at the Rose Bowl.

1984   *The Woman in Red* (movie soundtrack album) released. Detroit awards him its key to the city. Participates in recording of USA for Africa's "We Are the World." Appears as himself in episode of *The Cosby Show,* "Touch of Wonder."

1985   Wins Oscar for Best Song, "I Just Called to Say I Love You," from *The Woman in Red* soundtrack; dedicates the award to Nelson Mandela; in response, South African Broadcasting Corporation announces ban on his music March 26.

1989   Inducted into Rock 'N' Roll Hall of Fame.

1995   Appears in television documentary *The History of Rock 'n' Roll, Vol. 8:* "The 70's: Have a Nice Decade."

1997   Appears as himself in episode of television drama *New York Undercover,* "It's a Crime."

1999   Awarded $125,000 by Royal Swedish Academy of Music for Popular Music Prize, May 31; performs with Maya Angelou and others to open Special Olympics World Games in Raleigh, North Carolina, June 27. Grandson born to daughter Aisha, in October.

2000   Performs at celebration marking the opening of Desmond Tutu Peace Center in Cape Town, South Africa, held at the South African Consulate in New York City, June 13; becomes youngest recipient of a Kennedy Center Award, December 6.

DISCOGRAPHY

Albums

1962	*Jazz Soul of Little Stevie Wonder* *Tribute to Uncle Ray*
1963	*With a Song in My Heart* *Little Stevie Wonder: The 12-Year-Old Genius*
1964	*Call It Pretty Music* *Stevie at the Beach*
1965	*Stevie Wonder*
1966	*Down to Earth* *Uptight (Everything's Alright)*
1967	*I Was Made to Love Her* *Someday at Christmas*
1968	*For Once in My Life* *Eivets Rednow* *Greatest Hits*
1969	*My Cherie Amour*
1970	*Stevie Wonder Live* *Signed, Sealed & Delivered* *Talk of the Town*
1971	*Where I'm Coming From* *Stevie Wonder's Greatest Hits Volume 2*
1972	*Talking Book* *Music of My Mind*
1973	*Innervisions*
1974	*Fulfillingness' First Finale*
1976	*Portrait* *Songs in the Key of Life*
1978	*Looking Back*
1979	*Light My Fire* *Journey Through the Secret Life of Plants*
1980	*Hotter Than July*

1982	*Stevie Wonder's Original Musiquarium I*
1983	*Motown Legends*
1984	*The Woman in Red*
1985	*Love Songs* *In Square Circle*
1987	*Characters*
1995	*Conversation Peace* *Natural Wonder*
1999	*At the Close of the Century*

Compilations/Soundtracks

1994	*Shared Vision: Songs of the Beatles* *A Tribute to Curtis Mayfield*
1995	*The Music, the Magic, the Memories of Motown: A Tribute to Berry Gordy* *Inner City Blues: The Music of Marvin Gaye* *Soul Train 25th Anniversary Hall of Fame*
1996	*Mr. Holland's Opus* *Stealing Beauty*
1998	*Down in the Delta*
1999	*A Motown Christmas*

FURTHER READING

Crosby, David, and David Bender. *Stand and Be Counted: Making Music, Making History.* San Francisco: Harper, 1999.

Dragonwagon, C. *Stevie Wonder.* New York: Flash Books, 1977.

Elsner, Constanze. *Stevie Wonder.* New York: Popular Library, 1977.

Fox-Cumming, Ray. *Stevie Wonder.* Mankato, Minn.: Creative Education, 1975.

Haskins, Jim, and Kathleen Benson. *The Stevie Wonder Scrapbook.* New York: Grosset & Dunlap, 1978.

Sanford, William R., and Carl R. Green. *Center Stage: Stevie Wonder.* Mankato, Minn.: Crestwood House, 1986.

Shaw, Arnold. *The World of Soul.* New York: Cowles, 1970.

Taylor, Rick. *Stevie Wonder.* London: Omnibus, 1985.

White, Adam. *The Motown Story.* New York: Bedford Press, 1985.

Wilson, Beth P. *Stevie Wonder.* New York: Putnam, 1979.

Young, Al. *Bodies & Soul: Musical Memoirs.* Berkeley, Calif.: Berkeley Creative Arts Book Co., 1981.

APPENDIX

BLINDNESS-RELATED ORGANIZATIONS

American Brotherhood for the Blind
(a free lending library)
18840 Oxnard St.
Tarzana, CA 91356
Phone:(213) 343-2022

American Foundation for the Blind
11 Penn Plaza, Suite 300
New York, NY 10001
Phone: (212) 502-7600
         (800) 232-5463
Fax: (212) 502-7777
E-mail: afbinfo@afb.net

Better Vision for Children Foundation
916 Ocean Lane, Unit B
Imperial Beach, CA 91932
Phone: (619) 575-0214
E-mail: tresa@inetworld.net

Better Vision Institute
1800 North Kent St., Suite 1210
Rosslyn, VA 22209
Phone: (703) 243-1508

Braille Institute of America
741 North Vermont Ave.
Los Angeles, CA 90029
Phone: (323) 663-1111
         (800) 272-4553
E-mail: Info@BrailleInstitute.org
www.Brailleinstitute.org

Edith Bishel Center for the Blind and Visually Impaired
482 North Arthur St.
Kennewick, WA 99336
Phone: (509)735-0699
E-mail: ebc@tcfrn.org

The Hadley School for the Blind
700 Elm St.
Winnetka, IL 60093
Phone: (847) 446-8111
         (800) 323-4230
E-mail: info@hadley-school.org
www.hadley-school.org

Helen Keller Worldwide
90 West St., 2nd floor
New York, NY 10006
Phone: (212) 766-5266
Fax: (212) 791-7590
E-mail: info@hki.org
www.hki.org

Helen Keller National Center
111 Middleneck Rd.
Sands Point, NY 11050
Phone: (516) 944-8900

Howe Press
175 North Beacon St.
Watertown, MA 02172
Phone: (617) 924-3434

Lighthouse International
111 East 59th St.
New York, NY 10022
Phone: (212) 821-9200
         (800) 829-0500
Fax: (212) 821-9707
E-mail: info@lighthouse.org
www.lighthouse.org

Lions World Services for the Blind
2811 Fair Park Blvd.
Little Rock, AR 72143
Phone: (501) 664-7100
Fax: (501) 664-2743
E-mail: raining@lwsb.org
www.lwsb.org

Macular Degeneration Foundation
P.O. Box 9752
San Jose, CA 95157
Phone: (408) 260-1335
              (888) MDF-EYES (633-3937)

National Audio Theatre
P.O. Box 933
Hendersonville, NC
Phone: (828) 692-0621
E-mail: nat@wncguide.com

**National Association for Visually
    Handicapped**
22 West 21st St., 6th floor
New York, NY 10010
Phone: (212) 889-3141

National Braille Association, Inc.
Three Townline Circle
Rochester, NY 14623-2513
Phone: (716) 427-8260
Fax: (716) 427-0263

**National Eye Institute
National Institutes of Health**
Building 31, Room 6A32
Bethesda, MD 20892
Phone: (301) 496-5248

**National Library Service for the Blind
    and Physically Handicapped**
Library of Congress
1291 Taylor Street, NW
Washington, DC 20542
Phone: (202) 707-5100

**President's Committee on the Employment
    of People with Disabilities**
1331 F Street, NW
Washington, DC 20004-1107
Phone: (202) 376-6200
TDD: (202) 376-6205
Fax: (202) 376-6219

**Recording for the Blind and Dyslexic,
    Inc.**
20 Roszel Rd.
Princeton, NJ 08540
Phone: (609) 452-0606
              (800) 221-4792
Fax: (609) 987-8116
E-mail: webmaster@rfbd.org
www.rfbd.org

**SAP/Stevie Wonder Vision Awards:
    SAP America Inc.**
Strategic Planning and Support Office
3999 West Chester Pike
Newtown Square, PA 19073
http://www.sap.com/usa/

**T.M.T. Direct (Talk-Me-Thru Tutorials)—
    for computer use**
840 South Sheridan Blvd.
Denver, CO 80226
Phone: (888) 936-0001
E-mail: phil@redwhiteandblue.org

Equipment and Aids

Alphatek—talking watches, clocks,
    and calculators
1223 Wilshire Blvd., Suite 494
Santa Monica, CA 90403
Phone: (310) 393-7780

**Aster Synthetic Speech Application
    at Cornell University**
Ithaca, NY
Phone: (617) 621-6637
E-mail: raman@crl.dec.com

Cross Country Access
4799 Garreth Land
McKinney, TX 75070
Phone: (972) 562-3430
E-mail: avilon@cris.com
dJohnson2@adgrafix.com

Dolphin Computer Access LLC
100 South Ellsworth Ave.
4th Floor, Suites 48 & 49
San Mateo, CA 94401
Phone: (650) 348-7401
Fax: (650) 348-7403
E-mail: sales@dolphinusa.com

Humanware, Inc. (computer supplies)
6245 King Rd.
Loomis, CA 95650
Phone: (800) 722-3393
Fax: (916) 652-7296
E-mail: info@humanware.com

IBM Special Needs Solutions
11400 Burnet Rd.
Internal Zip 9448
Austin, TX 78758
Phone: (800) 426-4832
TDD: (800) 426-4833
Fax: (512) 838-9367
E-mail: snsinfo@austin.ibm.com

Microsystems Software, Inc.
600 Worcester Rd.
Framingham, MA 01702
Phone: (508) 416-1000
Fax: (508) 626-8515
E-mail: info@microsys.com

INDEX

PICTURE CREDITS

Page

3:   Globe Photos
10: Globe Photos
15: Associated Press, AP
17: Michael Ochs Archive
18: Photofest
25: Michael Ochs Archive
26: Michael Ochs Archive
31: Michael Ochs Archive
32: Photofest
34: Photofest

37: Photofest
41: Michael Ochs Archive
42: Michael Ochs Archive
45: Bettmann/Corbis
48: Photofest
50: Michael Ochs Archive
54: Photofest
56: Associated Press, AP
60: Associated Press, AP
63: Associated Press, AP

64: Associated Press, AP
68: Associated Press, AP
70: Associated Press, AP
73: Associated Press, AP
75: Associated Press, AP
78: Associated Press, AP
82: Mitchell Levy, Rangefinders, Globe Photos
86: Associated Press, AP

Cover Photos: Associated Press, AP; Reuters NewMedia Inc./Corbis

Tenley Williams has a Ph.D. in English from New York University. She lives in New York City, where she teaches literature and writing and is at work on a book about D. H. Lawrence.

James Scott Brady serves on the board of trustees with the Center to Prevent Handgun Violence and is the vice chairman of the Brain Injury Foundation. Mr. Brady served as assistant to the President and White House press secretary under President Ronald Reagan. He was severely injured in an assassination attempt on the president, but remained the White House press secretary until the end of the administration. Since leaving the White House, Mr. Brady has lobbied for stronger gun laws. In November 1993, President Bill Clinton signed the Brady Bill, a national law requiring a waiting period on handgun purchases and a background check on buyers.